About the Book

The Wright brothers wanted to build a flying machine from the time they were small boys. Most people thought they were crazy. But Wilbur and Orville said it could be done. While they were growing up, they made and flew hundreds of toy planes, kites, and gliders. Then they built an airplane with an engine. Finally, on December 17, 1903, at Kitty Hawk, their airplane flew. Here, in easy-to-read language, is the exciting story of the Wright brothers and their fantastic invention.

A SEE AND READ BEGINNING TO READ BIOGRAPHY

The Wright Brothers

BY CHARLES P. GRAVES

ILLUSTRATED BY FERMIN ROCKER

G. P. Putnam's Sons New York

For my niece and good companion
Anita Linzee Minot

SBN: GB-399-60790-0
SBN: TR-399-20303-6
Library of Congress Catalog Card Number: 72-81589
PRINTED IN THE UNITED STATES OF AMERICA
07209

One day the Wright brothers' father brought home a new toy. Wilbur was eleven, and Orville was seven. The year was 1878.

"Watch, boys," Mr. Wright said. He threw the toy above his sons' heads. The brothers shouted with delight as it flew up to the ceiling.

The flying toy was made of paper and light wood. It was powered by a twisted rubber band. Wilbur and Orville called it their bat. They played with it for many hours.

When the toy broke, the boys made some new "bats." The small ones they made flew very well. But the big ones did not.

From then on, the Wright brothers were very much interested in flying machines. At that time there were no airplanes and not even any cars. People traveled by train, ship, horse and buggy, and bicycle.

For hundreds of years, however, men had dreamed of flying. If birds can fly, men asked, why can't people?

Men and children, too, had tried to fly. They had made wings out of cloth or feathers and tied them to their arms. Then they jumped off high places, flapping their wings.

Crash! They hit the ground. Many were hurt.

About ninety years before the Wright brothers were born, men learned to go up in balloons. But the balloons were dangerous. They could catch fire. And when the Wrights were boys, there was no way to steer them. They could only drift with the wind.

The Wright boys never made a toy flying balloon, but they often played with kites. Orville's kites usually flew higher than those of his friends. He made kites and sold them for pocket money.

The Wrights lived in a house in Dayton, Ohio. Their father was a minister. When the boys were young, Mr. Wright worked in Indiana and Iowa for a time. But the boys always called Dayton their real home.

Wilbur was born in Indiana in 1867. Orville was born in Dayton four years later. They had two much older brothers and one younger sister.

Mrs. Wright's father had been a carriage maker and known for his fine work. Mrs. Wright was good at making things, too. She made household tools for herself. Once she made a sled and gave it to her sons for Christmas. The family said she "could mend anything."

From the time they were little, Wilbur and Orville loved to tinker with tools themselves. They made toy wagons and a telegraph set. Wilbur even made a machine to fold paper.

Orville was full of fun. Once he tried to make chewing gum out of tar and sugar. He thought he could sell it to his friends. When they tried it out, they became sick. That was the end of the chewing gum business!

When Orville was eleven, he was given a small printing press. With a friend, Ed Sines, he started an eighth-grade newspaper. They called it *The Midget.* One story read:

> Next week we propose to publish one of Miss Jenkins' famous lectures before the pupils of the Intermediate School on the Inherent Wickedness of School Children.

Luckily for the boys, the issue never came out. Miss Jenkins might have been angry.

Orville was a good printer. He began printing cards and posters and other things for money.

Soon he wanted a bigger press. He decided to build one. He learned how by reading books. Orville never had so much fun as when making the press. He used a gravestone as a "bed" to put the paper on.

When he was seventeen, Orville decided to build a press that was even bigger. Wilbur helped him. They cut some firewood into boards. They found pieces of iron in a junkyard. Wilbur had some good ideas for new ways to build a press. The press worked so well a printer from a big newspaper came to see it.

The brothers began printing a weekly newspaper. It carried neighborhood news. Wilbur was a good writer and wrote most of the stories.

When Orville finished school, the brothers put out a daily paper. They never went to college. But they learned a lot by doing and by reading. Wilbur especially loved reading. The brothers read any books they could find on science and invention.

There was a new invention then, the safety bicycle. Old bicycles had had one big high wheel and one little one. The new bikes had wheels of about the same size. They were very popular. The boys each bought one. Both brothers had always loved sports.

Orville began to enter bicycle races around Dayton. What fun it was to whiz around the track!

The Wright brothers decided to go into the bicycle business. They opened a shop in 1893. They sold bicycles. And they fixed old ones. Later they decided to make bicycles too. Theirs were well made and cheaper than most. Boys and girls were happy to buy them.

At this time the automobile was a new invention. A friend of the Wrights built the first one in Dayton. It didn't work very well and kept breaking down. But it was exciting to watch.

Orville thought there might be a big future for the automobile. Perhaps they should go into the automobile business, he told Wilbur.

"No," Wilbur said, shaking his head. He thought that building a good automobile would be almost impossible. "Why, it would be easier to build a flying machine," he said.

Recently some people had been experimenting with gliders. These are airplanes without engines. The wind keeps them up in the air. Most of the gliders had failed, and the inventors had given up. Still, scientists were beginning to think that flying machines, heavier than air, could be made successfully. (Balloons are filled with hot air, or gas, that is lighter than regular air. That is why they stay up.)

The Wright brothers read about a man in Germany named Otto Lilienthal. He had built a glider with wings shaped a little like a butterfly. He had sailed through the air from the top of a hill.

Orville and Wilbur thought that gliding must be the most wonderful sport in the world. They were sad when Lilienthal was killed in a glider crash.

The brothers wanted to work with gliders. They would carry on where Lilienthal had left off. They knew there was a lot to be done. Even Lilienthal's gliders had stayed in the air only a few seconds.

They started reading everything they could about flying. But there were few good flying books in the Dayton Library.

Wilbur wrote to a big museum in Washington, called the Smithsonian Institution. He knew that some men there were trying to learn to fly. Wilbur asked the museum for help. In his letter Wilbur said, "I believe that simple flight at least is possible for man."

The Smithsonian Institution lent the brothers some books. And the head of the museum, Samuel P. Langley, sent them some of his papers about flying. Langley, too, believed flying was possible.

Wilbur and Orville read the books and the papers. They found them helpful. But they did not agree with everything in them.

The brothers decided Lilienthal had crashed because he did not know how to control his glider. He had tried to balance it by moving his body about. This was too clumsy and unsure a way.

How could an airplane be properly balanced? the brothers asked themselves. How could it be made to go up and down and turned to the left and right? Wilbur and Orville realized they had to solve these problems if they were to build a flying machine that would really work.

They spent many hours talking about balance and control. One brother would have one idea, one another. Sometimes they argued.

The wings should be movable at the ends, they finally decided. One wing could be twisted up, the other down. Then the wings would meet the air at different angles. As a result, one would get greater lift from the air than the other. This would make it possible to balance and steer the plane. There should be a rudder, too, they realized, to help the plane change its direction. As on a boat, the rudder would be a flat piece attached to the back. By moving it from side to side, the glider could be steered.

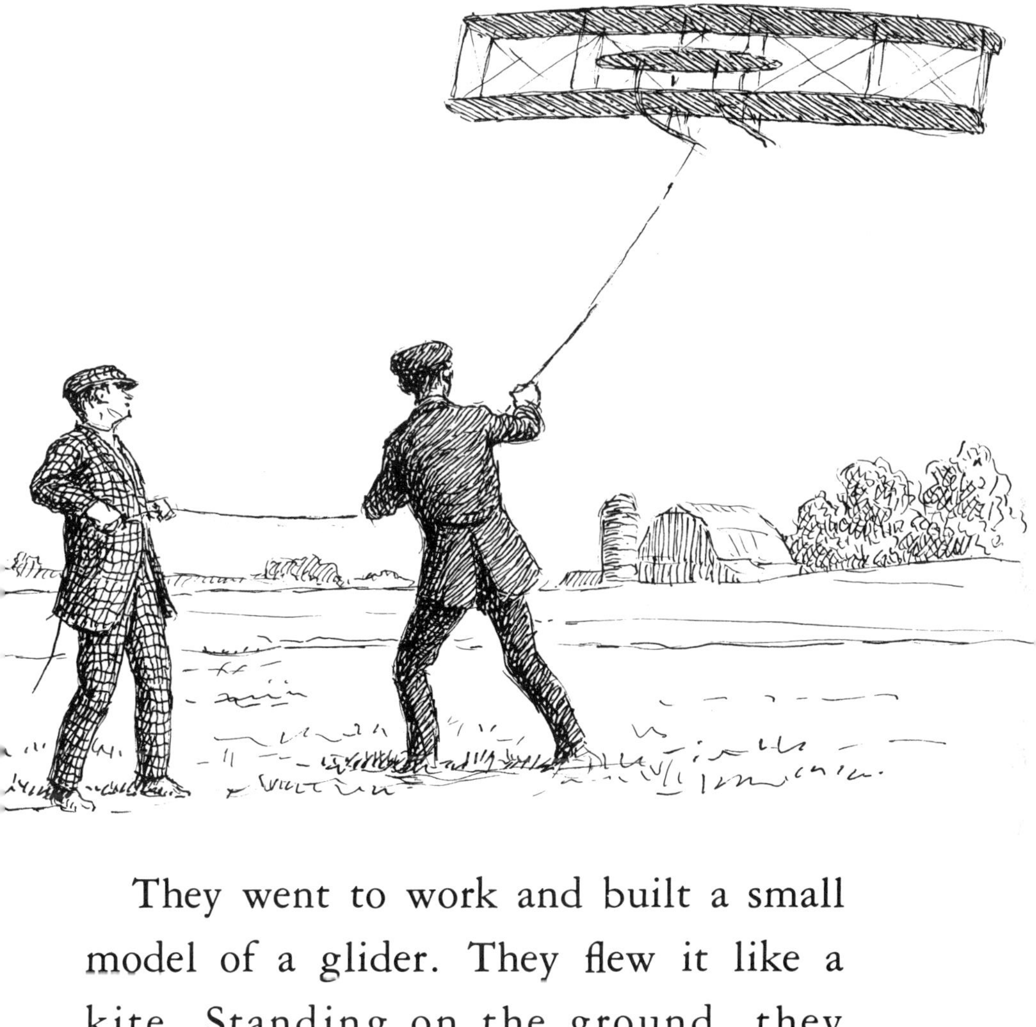

They went to work and built a small model of a glider. They flew it like a kite. Standing on the ground, they worked the controls by pulling on ropes. The model flew very well.

Wilbur and Orville were excited. They felt sure they could build a glider big enough to carry a man.

In September, 1900, their big glider was finished. Soon they took it to Kitty Hawk. This was a tiny fishing village by the sea in North Carolina. They had picked Kitty Hawk because the winds there were strong. A glider needs strong winds to stay aloft. Also, Kitty Hawk was very flat and sandy. There were few trees to get in the way during flight.

The Wright brothers camped in a tent on the sand. Orville did most of the cooking. Sometimes they shot game. Then they had wild goose, or fish hawk, or squirrel for supper.

At first, the Wrights flew their glider like a big kite. After they had practiced steering it, they took it to a big sand dune. It was named Kill Devil Hill. They took turns gliding from the top.

Their glider had two wings. The flier lay on the bottom wing as the glider went through the air. The other brother watched and made notes about how the glider was working. They kept fixing the controls in different ways to try to make them work better.

At times the glider got out of control and landed with a crash. But the sand was soft, and neither brother was hurt badly. When parts of the glider broke, they were able to fix them.

The Wrights went home to Dayton in late August. That winter they worked in their bicycle shop to earn money. They also made a much larger glider. Its wings were more curved than before. They believed this would help it lift better in the wind.

The next summer they went back to Kitty Hawk. They made more flights with their new glider. Sometimes they flew almost 400 feet. Each time they learned more about control.

They took an even bigger and better glider to Kitty Hawk the following summer. Their new plane had a tail. They flew it more than a thousand times. Now they felt sure that powered flight was possible. All that was needed was a small motor. It would drive the plane through the air with propellers. As the blades of the propellers spun, more and more air would be pushed behind them. The plane would move ahead to where the air was thinner.

If the plane went through the air fast enough, the air pressure below the wings would become greater than that above. The air below would then push the plane up.

The Wright brothers went to work on a gasoline engine when they got home. Their engine had to be powerful, they knew, yet not too heavy. The propellers had to be just the right size for the plane. And they had to hit the air at the right angle. What was the right size for the engine and the propellers? They would have to find out.

Gasoline engines were new then. Even the automobile companies could give the brothers little help. For ideas about propellers, they studied propellers on ships.

Wilbur and Orville talked and talked, trying to figure out what would work best. Each improved on the other's ideas.

They took the parts of their flying machine to Kitty Hawk in September, 1903. Wilbur was thirty-six by then, and Orville thirty-two. Would they be the first men to fly in a powered airplane? Samuel P. Langley of the Smithsonian Institution had also just finished making a flying machine.

While they worked putting their plane together, they heard about Langley. A man had tried to fly his airplane twice. Each time he had failed.

The Wrights tested their engine. Now they had a new worry. Some parts were not strong enough. They had to rebuild them. The weather was getting cold, making their work harder.

Finally, on December 14, 1903, everything was ready. And the wind was just right. The brothers tossed a coin to see who would be the first to try the flying machine. Wilbur won.

The plane raced down a small track they had laid on the sand. Into the air it went, under its own power. But Wilbur turned it upward too quickly. The engine stalled. Down it came after only three and one-half seconds.

The plane was hurt landing. But the brothers were not discouraged. They felt sure their airplane would fly. They had complete faith they had built it so it would. All they needed was practice controlling it.

They telegraphed their father: "Power and control ample. Rudder only injured. Success assured."

They mended the airplane. Then on Thursday, December 17, they were ready to try it again. Men from the Kill Devil Lifesaving Station came to watch. A small boy stood with them, his eyes wide with excitement.

Orville climbed into the plane. He started the motor and let it warm up. Slowly, the plane began to move. Wilbur ran alongside it, steadying a wing with one hand. Suddenly the plane rose into the air. A man from the lifesaving station took a picture.

It was very windy, and Orville had a hard time controlling the airplane. The flying machine stayed in the air only twelve seconds and went only 100 feet. But Orville was very happy. It was the first powered flight in history made by a man.

Now it was Wilbur's turn to fly the airplane. He stayed in the air a little longer than Orville had. Orville made a third flight. This time he, too, did better. He was more practiced now at handling the plane.

Afterward Wilbur made a fourth flight. He stayed up almost a minute and went 852 feet.

It was a great day for the Wright brothers. They sent another telegram to their father: "Success four flight. . . . Inform press. Home Christmas."

Surprisingly enough, there was little excitement about the flight. Few newspapers printed the story. People just couldn't believe that two unknown bicycle makers had built an airplane that would really fly.

But the Wrights worked on building bigger and better planes. In 1905, they made a flight of 24 miles!

Before long they were world-famous. People everywhere began to realize how useful airplanes could be. Airplanes could carry people, mail, and supplies. They could be used in war. And they could be used for exploration.

Men in Europe and the United States built planes using the Wrights' ideas. The Wrights themselves went into the airplane business.

Wilbur did not enjoy his fame for long. He died in 1912 from typhoid fever.

Orville was brokenhearted, but he went on working. He lived till 1948. He lived to see huge airplanes circle the world and millions of people fly each year.

After the Wright brothers became famous, people would ask their father which did the most work inventing the airplane. He replied, "About equal credit is due each."

Wilbur and Orville looked alike, thought alike, and worked alike. They always worked as a team. "They are as inseparable as twins," Mr. Wright said.

Their invention made them rich as well as famous. But what Orville and Wilbur enjoyed the most was the fun of building an airplane that worked. Their first powered plane may be seen today in the Smithsonian Institution in Washington.

Key Words

airplane
automobile
balance
bat
bicycle
blade
control
crash
engine
gasoline
glider
invention
machine
minister
museum
powered
pressure
propeller
rudder
science
steer
telegraph

Other Biographies in the *See and Read* Series

Booker T. Washington *by William Wise*
Illustrated by Paul Frame

Robert Fulton *by Ruby L. Radford*
Illustrated by Salem Tamer

Thomas Alva Edison *by Patricia Miles Martin*
Illustrated by Fermin Rocker

Marie Curie *by Lorraine Henriod*
Illustrated by Fermin Rocker

Henry Ford *by Adrian A. Paradis*
Illustrated by Paul Frame

Matthew A. Henson *by Charles P. Graves*
Illustrated by Ronald Dorfman

Richard E. Byrd *by Helen D. Olds*
Illustrated by Frank Aloise

The Author

Charles P. Graves was born and educated in Florida. Following a varied writing career, including jobs in advertising, newspapers, and radio, he authored more than twenty children's books. Many were biographies of famous Americans, among them *See and Read Biographies* of Frederick Douglass, Matthew A. Henson, and Mark Twain published by Putnam. Mr. Graves died shortly after completing *The Wright Brothers.*

The Artist

Fermin Rocker was born in London, England, and received his art training in Berlin, Germany. After coming to America, he worked as a commercial artist drawing animated cartoons. His graphics, watercolors, and oil paintings have been frequently exhibited and won the artist several awards. Mr. Rocker and his family have recently moved to England.